THE
SAN FRANCISCO
EARTHQUAKE
of 1906

A HISTORY PERSPECTIVES BOOK

Marcia Amidon Lusted

Published in the United States of America
by Cherry Lake Publishing
Ann Arbor, Michigan
www.cherrylakepublishing.com

Consultants: Lisa A. Wald, Geophysicist, U.S. Geological Survey, Golden, Colorado; Marla
Conn, ReadAbility, Inc.
Editorial direction: Red Line Editorial
Book design: Sleeping Bear Press

Photo Credits: Library of Congress, cover, 7, 9; Underwood & Underwood/Library of
Congress, cover; Arnold Genthe/Library of Congress, cover, 20, 29; Currier & Ives/Library
of Congress, 4; AP Images, 5; Harris & Ewing, Inc./Library of Congress, 12; Bettmann/
Corbis/AP Images, 14; Bettmann/Corbis, 16, 25; C.L. Wasson/International Stereoscopic
Co./Library of Congress, 18; H.C. White Co./Library of Congress, 22; Ted Streshinsky/
Corbis, 27; Detroit Publishing Company/Library of Congress, 30

Library of Congress Cataloging-in-Publication Data
Lüsted, Marcia Amidon.
  The San Francisco earthquake of 1906 / Marcia Amidon Lusted.
     pages cm. -- (Perspectives library)
  Includes bibliographical references and index.
  ISBN 978-1-63137-619-1 (hardcover) -- ISBN 978-1-63137-664-1 (pbk.)
-- ISBN 978-1-63137-709-9 (pdf ebook) -- ISBN 978-1-63137-754-9 (ebook)
1. San Francisco Earthquake and Fire, Calif., 1906--Juvenile literature. 2. Earthquakes
--California--San Francisco--History--20th century--Juvenile literature. 3. Fires
--California--San Francisco--History--20th century--Juvenile literature.
4. San Francisco (Calif.)--History--20th century--Juvenile literature. I. Title.
F869.S357L87 2014
979.4'61051--dc23

                              2014004586

Cherry Lake Publishing would like to acknowledge the work of
The Partnership for 21st Century Skills. Please visit www.p21.org
for more information.

Printed in the United States of America
Corporate Graphics Inc.
July 2014

TABLE OF CONTENTS

In this book, you will read about the San Francisco Earthquake of 1906 from three perspectives. Each perspective is based on real things that happened to real people who lived in San Francisco at the time of the earthquake. You will see that the same event can look different depending on whose point of view you see it from.

1

John Morrill

Fireman

The first **jolt** knocked me out of my bed. I wasn't sure what was happening—then I realized it was an earthquake. I thought the firehouse was going to fall down around me. I am a fireman for the San Francisco Fire Department. My firehouse is the 30th Engine Company. It is located on Waller Street, not far from Golden Gate Park. I work 21 hours at a time and live at the firehouse when I am on duty.

It was only shortly after 5:00 a.m. I yelled to Samuel, a fellow fireman. "Earthquake! The building is falling down!" He quickly scrambled across the floor. I am a San Francisco native, born and bred. I am no stranger to earthquakes. But this one was like nothing I had ever felt before. I was on the second floor of our building. The floor beneath my feet was shaking up and down and side to side. It was difficult to stand up.

I stumbled to the fire pole and grabbed it to slide down to the ground floor. The opening for the pole was moving and the pole was bent. I was afraid I'd be

*The shaking ground opened up cracks in the **cobblestone** streets.* ▶

crushed. Samuel and I both tumbled down the corkscrew stairs instead.

We staggered out to the street. Dust filled the air. Pieces of brick and cement fell from buildings onto the street. The street's cobblestones rose and fell as if they floated on water. A large crack opened up in the middle of the street. It was six feet deep and half-filled with water. A man passed us, bleeding from a wound on his head. He was clearly shocked and confused. Dodging more falling bricks, I ran to him and pulled him into the doorway of another building where he was safe from falling debris.

Then I went back to help Samuel with the horses. They were whinnying and stamping in terror. We led them from the firehouse and then hitched them to the fire

SECOND SOURCE

▶ Find a second source from someone who experienced the first few moments of the earthquake. Compare the information there to the information in this source.

wagon. I could smell the sharp tang of smoke in the air. I could hear yelling and screaming. Slowly the **tremors** under my feet stilled. Shaking continued off and on for days. These were the earthquake's **aftershocks**.

▲ *Firefighters relied on horses to quickly bring fire wagons to fires in 1906.*

More of our fellow firefighters joined us. We set off in the wagon toward the Haight-Ashbury district of the city. We saw the first **tendrils** of smoke in the air near there. Samuel, another firefighter named Freddy, and I stopped the horses near a building where we could see flames. We tried to connect our hoses to a hydrant. No water came out—not a drop.

"The water pipes have broken!" Freddy yelled. All we had was the water in our wagon's tank. We began spraying it on a five-story hotel, which had collapsed onto itself. It reminded me of a telescope. Each floor had collapsed onto the one below it until the fifth floor was at street level. Flames hungrily licked at the window frames. I could hear the frantic voices of people trapped inside as the flames and heat grew closer. We were only able to help a few of them escape before the fire got too hot.

I would not see the firehouse again for many days. I later learned it had served as both a hospital

▲ *The Palace Hotel in downtown San Francisco was destroyed by fire after surviving the earthquake's first shocks.*

and **morgue**. I never slept more than an hour at a time. There was little to eat or drink. I traveled from fire to fire, helplessly trying to put out flames without water. Sometimes we used dirt or sand. Other times we set smaller fires that we hoped would burn toward the existing fires. We thought the new fires would use up the oxygen and fuel needed by the bigger fires. Sadly, it did not usually work. Finally we tried using dynamite. A man who worked blasting tunnels for the Southern Pacific Railroad had a truckload of dynamite. We wanted to blow up buildings to create a **firebreak** that the flames could not pass. I wasn't sure that blowing up buildings was the best option, but what choice did we have? We were fighting fires without water, equipment, or enough men.

THINK ABOUT IT

▶ Determine the main point of this paragraph. Pick out a piece of evidence that supports it.

The city boomed with the sound of dynamite and falling buildings. Flames, smoke, and dust blanketed the city. But we could not stop the fires that consumed San Francisco. By the time it was over, three days later, I knew the fires had done much more damage than the earthquake itself. And as a fireman, I felt as if I had been powerless to save my city.

WHY DYNAMITE?

Firemen thought dynamite might create zones that fire could not cross. In the destroyed zones, there were no buildings that could burn. Without fuel, firefighters hoped the fires would burn out. Unfortunately, at times the dynamite merely set buildings on fire.

2

Sophie Charles
Russian Hill Resident

As long as I can remember, I've lived in our beautiful white house on top of Russian Hill in San Francisco, California. From here I can look out over the city, but our green slopes and cliffs separate us from it too. It was always peaceful in our neighborhood. But everything changed on Wednesday morning, April 18, 1906. It was just two days after my twelfth birthday.

Papa woke me up early that morning. I couldn't understand why my room seemed to be moving. Papa had trouble standing up. He pulled me from my bed and down the stairs. "It's an earthquake, Sophie," he yelled. I stumbled behind him with sleep still clouding my eyes. Mama was right behind us, holding baby Jamie in her arms. Lucinda was clutching the back of Mama's nightgown. We all nearly tumbled onto our green lawn. It was so odd that the ground under my feet did not stop moving. There did not seem to be any safe place to stand.

Our neighbors gathered outside as well. We watched as bricks tumbled off chimneys and trees seemed to rip their own roots from the ground. But we were thankful that everyone in our neighborhood escaped safely and that no one's home seemed to be badly damaged. "Perhaps it's

ANALYZE THIS

▶ Analyze two accounts of experiencing the earthquake in this book. How are they the same? How are they different?

▲ *The residents of Russian Hill watched the fires burning in the city below.*

because we live on a hill," Papa noted, "and not on the land closer to the bay." That land was built up by dumping soil onto **wetlands**. Papa told us it was not very stable.

As we all gazed out over the city below, we could see the smoke rising in twisting columns from the ruins. Soon orange flames were visible as well. For the next three days, the fire spread out below us. Choking smoke and **cinders** reached the hill and Papa and the other men worked tirelessly to put them out. There was a terrible, bitter smell in the air that made my stomach churn. Mama shooed me into the house and said it was simply the smell of burning buildings, but I later overheard her talking to Mrs. Livermore in a hushed voice. She said that it was also the smell of death in the city's ruins.

By Friday we thought the fires were out and our homes had escaped both earthquake and flames. Mama even thought about putting back the

▲ *A woman held her nose while walking past ruined buildings, as the smell was strong after the fires in the city.*

valuables and supplies that she'd placed next to the door in case we needed to escape quickly. But as Papa and I stood in the garden, which looked down on Van Ness Avenue, we heard a dull thump of an explosion followed by a cloud of dust and debris. "They've dynamited the Viavi Company!" Papa yelled.

"Why would they dynamite a building now, when it survived the earthquake and fire?" I asked, puzzled.

"Because they think it will keep another fire from starting inside the wooden building," Papa told me as he set off running for the Livermore's house. "But it's a patent medicine company! There are thousands of gallons of alcohol there." Even I knew that alcohol burns easily. I stared, unable to look away, as bright flames shot up from the ruins.

Once again our beautiful neighborhood on Russian Hill was being threatened by fire. Papa and many of the other men fought the cinders and sparks that drifted up the hill and landed on roofs and fences. A spark had set Mr. Livermore's shed on fire, where he kept his coal. The men used water

THINK ABOUT IT

▶ Determine the main point of this chapter. Pick out one piece of evidence that supports it.

from the lily pond in his garden to put it out. If the coal had caught fire, the fire would have easily spread to other nearby buildings. Mr. Livermore's son Norman stamped out a patch of grass burning not ten inches from their house!

Then the soldiers came. They ordered us to leave our houses. Papa and the other men argued with them. But the soldiers wouldn't listen. They pointed their rifles at Mr. Richardson and his wife, forcing them to leave. They even threatened to shoot Mr. Jenks, who was up on the roof of his

◀ *Soldiers take a break from patrolling the ruined city of San Francisco, where they tried to maintain order.*

home putting out sparks. Mama, Jamie, Lucinda, and I had to leave, but Papa and many other men crept back secretly to keep Russian Hill from burning like the rest of San Francisco. It was only because of Papa and the other men that our homes were still standing when we came back the next day. I am very proud of my neighbors and how they worked together to save Russian Hill.

PATROLLING RUSSIAN HILL

Soldiers were called into San Francisco immediately after the earthquake. It was their job to prevent people from looting and stealing. They also helped evacuate residents and dynamite buildings to try to stop the spread of fires. Sometimes soldiers threatened people to make them leave their homes.

3

Chuen Lee
Man from Chinatown

My name is Chuen Lee. For all of my 15 years, I have lived in San Francisco. But if someone actually asked me where I was from, I would say Chinatown. It's like living in a city within a city. My parents came here from China and opened a shop where they sell Chinese foods and medicines. My brother and I were born here, but we rarely speak or hear a language other than Chinese and we don't leave Chinatown very often. It is my home. And since most people in San Francisco are either afraid of us or think poorly of us, who can blame the Chinese for remaining separate from the Americans? They really want our land in Chinatown, which is some of the best in the city.

When I was thrown out of my bed early on April 18, my first thought was that the officials of San Francisco had decided to level Chinatown and drive us all out. But I quickly realized it was an earthquake. We had felt them before. Mother was crying, claiming that the Earth Dragon was

ANALYZE THIS

▶ Analyze another account of a resident of Chinatown who experienced the earthquake. Compare it with this account. How are the two accounts different? How are they the same?

▲ *Much of Chinatown was completely destroyed by the earthquake.*

angry and was splitting the cobblestones and shaking the ground beneath us. As we made our way outside, we could also see that the Fire Dragon was spitting flames at many of the buildings around us. Father said that it was the end of the world and we needed to get to the temple and offer **incense** to appease the dragons. Then I saw a bull running loose in the streets, and Mother collapsed. She moaned that it was a bad omen. She thought it was clearly one of the four bulls in Chinese mythology that held up the world on their backs.

There was no time to reach the temple. We were forced to grab what we could from the shop and flee Chinatown. My brother and I dragged a wooden box with as much food as we could carry. Mother and Father carried bedding and any other household goods they were able to find as our house was beginning to smolder. I could smell scorched wood and see flames licking at the roof.

We headed west toward the Presidio fort and Golden Gate Park along with crowds of other Chinese. Soon we were joined by all kinds of people: Chinese, Japanese, Africans, Spanish, and many more. We were all oddly silent. The only sound was the scraping of trunks and boxes on the pavement. Then suddenly the ground shook again and there was an explosion. It was different from the shaking of aftershocks. We stopped and looked behind us. I asked Father what it was.

"They are dynamiting our buildings," Father told me grimly. "They use black powder, though, which will only feed the Fire Dragon." Father was right, because by the next day all of Chinatown was

▲ *Residents took what they could and left the city after the earthquake.*

THINK ABOUT IT

▶ Determine the main point of this chapter. Pick out one piece of evidence that supports it.

gone, flattened first by the earthquake and then by the fire. City officials had told us that we had to go to a Chinese-only **refugee** camp at the Presidio. Army soldiers gathered up other Chinese and forced them to the camp as well. It was cold and windy and we had to camp on the fort grounds with little protection. The rumor quickly spread that the city officials were going to use this opportunity to keep us from rebuilding Chinatown where it was.

And yet these efforts to make our Chinatown go away did not work. Our Chinese leaders convinced the city officials that they could rebuild Chinatown so it would be better than ever. It would have even more of a feeling of China

▲ *Many people had to stay in camps after their homes were destroyed.*

itself, in the buildings, architecture, and decoration. It would attract more business and tourists to San Francisco at a time when the city needed all the money it could get. The city officials agreed and we were eventually able to return to our home. The Earth Dragon was quiet again . . . for now.

CHINESE IMMIGRATION

In the early 1900s there was a strong anti-Chinese feeling in California. Many Americans thought Chinese workers were taking too many jobs. The Chinese Exclusion Act of 1882 was the first major U.S. law to restrict **immigration**. It focused on one nationality of people—the Chinese. This law stopped Chinese workers from coming to the United States. It also stopped many Chinese people from becoming U.S. citizens.

▲ *Chinatown was later rebuilt from its ruins.*

LOOK, LOOK AGAIN

Take a close look at this photograph of the ruins of San Francisco's City Hall after the earthquake. Then answer the following questions:

1. How would a fireman feel when he looked at this photograph? How would he feel about his role during the fire?

2. What would one of the residents of Russian Hill think when she saw this photograph and the condition of the rest of the city?

3. What would a resident of Chinatown tell his relatives in China about this image?

GLOSSARY

aftershock (AF-tur-shok) a smaller earthquake that follows a larger, main earthquake

cinder (SIN-dur) a small piece of partly burned wood that can still catch on fire

cobblestone (KOB-uhl-stone) a small round stone used to pave roads

firebreak (FIRE-brayk) an obstacle used to stop the spread of a fire

immigration (IM-i-gray-shun) moving to a new country that one is not originally from

incense (IN-senss) a spice or other substance that is burned to make a sweet smell

jolt (JOHLT) to move suddenly with rough jerks

morgue (MORG) a place where bodies are kept where they can be identified

refugee (ref-yuh-JEE) a person forced to leave his or her home to escape a natural disaster, war, or other problem

tendril (TEN-drel) a thin wisp or curl of something, such as smoke

tremor (TREM-ur) a shaking or violent movement

wetland (WET-land) land consisting of marshes or swamps with moist soil

LEARN MORE

Further Reading

Blundell, Judy. *Dear America: A City Tossed and Broken.* New York: Scholastic, 2013.
Slavicek, Louise Chipley. *The San Francisco Earthquake and Fire of 1906.* New York: Chelsea House, 2008.
Tarshis, Lauren. *I Survived the San Francisco Earthquake, 1906.* New York: Scholastic, 2012.

Web Sites

National Archives: San Francisco Earthquake, 1906
http://www.archives.gov/legislative/features/sf/
This Web site has information about the earthquake and photographs of the earthquake and fires that destroyed the city.

The San Francisco Earthquake, 1906
http://www.eyewitnesstohistory.com/sfeq.htm
On this Web site, read about the earthquake through the words of people who experienced it in 1906.

INDEX

ABOUT THE AUTHOR

Marcia Amidon Lusted has written more than 90 books and 400 magazine articles for young readers, many of them about U.S. history. She is also an associate editor and staff writer for Cobblestone Publishing. She lives in New Hampshire, where earthquakes don't happen very often.